First World War
and Army of Occupation
War Diary
France, Belgium and Germany

29 DIVISION
Divisional Troops
227 Machine Gun Company
12 July 1917 - 31 January 1918

WO95/2294/2

The Naval & Military Press Ltd
www.nmarchive.com
Published in association with The National Archives

Published by

The Naval & Military Press Ltd

Unit 10 Ridgewood Industrial Park,

Uckfield, East Sussex,

TN22 5QE England

Tel: +44 (0) 1825 749494

www.naval-military-press.com

www.nmarchive.com

This diary has been reprinted in facsimile from the original. Any imperfections are inevitably reproduced and the quality may fall short of modern type and cartographic standards.

© **Crown Copyright**
Images reproduced by permission of The National Archives, London, England, 2015.

Contents

Document type	Place/Title	Date From	Date To
Heading	WO95/2294 29 Div 227 Machine Gun Coy July 1917-Jan 1918		
Heading	29th Division Divl Troops 227th Machine Gun Coy Jly 1917-1918 Jan		
War Diary	Le Havre	12/07/1917	18/07/1917
War Diary	Proven	19/07/1917	20/07/1917
Heading	War Diary Of 227 Coy. Machine Gun Corps From Aug 1st 1917 To Aug 31st 1917 (Volume 2)		
War Diary	Proven	01/08/1917	06/08/1917
War Diary	Proven & Field	07/08/1917	07/08/1917
War Diary	Field	08/08/1917	26/08/1917
War Diary	Proven	27/08/1917	31/08/1917
Miscellaneous	29th Division M.G. Barrage Instructions App I		
Miscellaneous	29th Division M.G. Barrage		
Miscellaneous	War Diary Of 227 Coy. Machine Gun Corps From 1-9-1917 To 30-9-1917 (Volume III)		
Miscellaneous	From O.C. 227 Coy M.G.C. To D.H.Q. 29th Division	01/10/1917	01/10/1917
War Diary	Proven	01/09/1917	21/09/1917
War Diary	Field	22/09/1917	30/09/1917
Miscellaneous	Appendix Company Orders By Captain J.W. Davis. Cmdg 227 M.G. Coy	20/09/1917	20/09/1917
Heading	War Diary Of 227 Coy. Machine Gun Corps From 1/10/1917 To 31/10/1917 (Volume IV)		
Miscellaneous	From O.C. 227 Coy M.G.C. To D.H.Q. 29th Division	02/11/1917	02/11/1917
War Diary Diagram etc	Field	01/10/1917	31/10/1917
Heading	War Diary Of 227 Coy Machine Gun Corps From 1/11/17 To 30/11/17 (Volume V)		
Miscellaneous	From O.C. 227 Coy M.G.C. To D.H.Q. 29th Division	15/11/1917	15/11/1917
War Diary	Field	01/11/1917	11/11/1917
War Diary	Hendicourt	12/11/1917	17/11/1917
War Diary	Haut Allaines	18/11/1917	18/11/1917
War Diary	Fins	19/11/1917	20/11/1917
War Diary	Marcoing	21/11/1917	30/11/1917
Heading	War Diary Of 227 Machine Gun Company From 1/12/17 To 31/12/17 (Volume VI)		
Miscellaneous	From O.C. 227 Coy M.G.C. To D.H.Q. 29th Division	31/12/1917	31/12/1917
War Diary	Marcoing	01/12/1917	04/12/1917
War Diary	Fins	05/12/1917	05/12/1917
War Diary	Grand Roullecourt	06/12/1917	07/12/1917
War Diary	Denier	08/12/1917	17/12/1917
War Diary	Blangerval	18/12/1917	18/12/1917
War Diary	Vieil Hesdin	19/12/1917	19/12/1917
War Diary	Fruges	20/12/1917	20/12/1917
War Diary	Clenleu	21/12/1917	31/12/1917
War Diary	Devlein	01/01/1918	04/01/1918
War Diary	Westebecourt	05/01/1918	16/01/1918
War Diary	Brandhoek	17/01/1918	17/01/1918
War Diary	Ypres	18/01/1918	24/01/1918
War Diary	Wieltje	26/01/1918	31/01/1918

WO 95/2294
29 Div
227 machine gun Coy   July 1917 - Jan 1918

29TH DIVISION
DIVL TROOPS

~~29 Bn. M.G. Corps~~
~~Formerly~~
227TH MACHINE GUN COY
JLY 1917 - ~~DECEMBER~~ OCT 1919

1918 JAN

2069 + 2084

227 M.G. Coy
M G Corps

Vol I

Day 17
to
Dec 16

WAR DIARY or INTELLIGENCE SUMMARY
Army Form C. 2118.

Place	Date	Hour	Summary of Events and Information	Remarks and references to Appendices

Le Havre LE HAVRE	12/4/17		Company disembarked at LE HAVRE with 225, 226, & 228 Coys
			Strength. O C Company Capt J W DAVIS
			2/Lt Capt C C BAMBER C.S.M. 162104 J.M. ODLUM
			No.1 Section {2/Lt R W HUNTER C.Q.M.S 58805 C.Q.M.S. SMITH
			              {2/Lt W RICHARDS
			No 2 Section {2/Lt R J MATTHEWS. Officers Rk & File Riding Horses
			              {2/Lt J KINAHAN. 10 177 +3 9
			No 3 Section {2/Lt W M GEGGIE. Addition of 1 A.S.C. Private with coy
			              {2/Lt H J WADHAM. 1 G S Wagon
			No 4 Section {2/Lt A J BRIDGMAN. 2 H D. Horses
			              {2/Lt D S McGREGOR
			Transport officer
			Company marched up to Rest Camp I Section A
			Capt DAVIS appointed O C Wing. O.C.Coys expected
			to Camp Commandant to receive Routine & other orders regarding
			to inspections etc & replacement of deficiencies etc
			C C Bamber Capt	

Army Form C. 2118.

WAR DIARY
or
INTELLIGENCE SUMMARY.
(Erase heading not required.)

Instructions regarding War Diaries and Intelligence Summaries are contained in F. S. Regs., Part II. and the Staff Manual respectively. Title pages will be prepared in manuscript.

Place	Date	Hour	Summary of Events and Information	Remarks and references to Appendices
LE HAVRE	13/9/17		The Company was "Coy on Duty". The day was occupied by kit inspection. Camp Commandant inspected camp at 11 a.m. Stores & equipment were drawn from O. Stores at the docks. 4 water carts for drawing 4 mules each at SOUTHAMPTON sent by wire. Strength O. 10 O.R. 177 + 1. A.S.C. Driver (attd) Animals Riding 7 Mules 43 H.D.2. Sick O.R. 2.	
LE HAVRE	14/9/17		Company continued with inspection of equipment & gun gear & took of deficiencies made. All deficiencies drawn from Ordnance Stores. The Docks. Camp Commandants Inspection of lines 11 a.m. Baking Parade 2 p.m. Strength O. 10 O.R. 177 + 1 A.S.C. Driver (attd) Animals Riding 7 Mules 43 from Remounts 4. H.D.2. Sick O.R. 6.	
LE HAVRE	15/9/17		Church Parade 9 a.m. Y.M.C.A. - no padre. No Commandants Inspection. Baking 2 p.m. O.C. Company inspected all cleanliness & arrangements in lines. Strength O. 10 O.R. 178. Animals Riding 7, H.D.2. Mules 47. Sick O.R. 3.	

C. C. Bambridge /st

WAR DIARY
or
INTELLIGENCE SUMMARY.
(Erase heading not required.)

Army Form C. 2118.

Place	Date	Hour	Summary of Events and Information	Remarks and references to Appendices
LE HAVRE	16/7/17		Physical Training 9 a.m – 10 a.m Rifle Inspection 10 a.m Bathing Parade 2 p.m. Stand Easy a/c at Ox 9 Co E 9-10 equivalent 796 P.S. 56 from P.R.I. CLIPSTONE.	
LE HAVRE	17/7/17		Parades 8 a.m – 9 a.m Cleaning up Lines 9 a.m Inspection of Lines by O.C. Coy 9.15 a.m – 10.15 a.m Rifle Inspection & Squad Drill 10.30 – 11.30 a.m Elementary Gun Drill 11.30 – 12.30 p.m Care & Cleaning of Gun 2 p.m – 3 p.m All N.C.O's Lime Direction Future Strengths by T.S. Use of A.A.M	
			Orders received for entraining at GARE des MARCHAND Point 3. Appendix of orders received attached c.c.Rm. 'SES	
LE HAVRE	18/7/17		Marched off from Rest Camp I. Section A 10.30 a.m Entrained 12. noon Quick entrainment Cyst ablated by R.T.O. Left 2 p.m Route. BUCHY Rest 1 hr — ABBEVILLE — HAZEBROUCK — POPERINGHE. Strength 10 Off. 175 O.R. 7 Riding 47 Mules 2 A.D. 2 days Rations on Train. Appendix of Route & Order attached.	

Army Form C. 2118.

WAR DIARY
or
INTELLIGENCE SUMMARY.
(Erase heading not required.)

Instructions regarding War Diaries and Intelligence Summaries are contained in F.S. Regs., Part II. and the Staff Manual respectively. Title pages will be prepared in manuscript.

Place	Date	Hour	Summary of Events and Information	Remarks and references to Appendices
PROVEN.	19/4/17.	9.15 a.m.	Arrived at Railhead HOPOUTRE – POPERINGHE. (Maj. HAZEBROUCK S.A.) Met by Div. M.G. Officer who took ½ O/c on by Car to proposed Camping Area. Coy became divorced M.G. Coy to 29 Div. XIV Corps on 15. Div. XIV Corps Div. y 35 Div 29 Div. K Bns. owing to relief taking place between 29 Div y 35 Div K Bn. coming out of line. There was some difficulty about tracks camping ground in Coy "M" lines came into march camp who accorded hut in Central Camp. PROVEN. y Ridng Horses 47 Mules 2 A.D. Strength 10 Officers 175 O.R. No sick.	
PROVEN.	20/4/17		Parades. Reveille 6.30 a.m. Rifle & Gas Helmet Inspection 10 a.m. Breakfast 7.15 a.m. Shaving & Dressing 10.30 a.m. Inspection of huts 9 a.m. 1 issue of Ammunition & Iron Rations Lect Inspection 9.30 a.m. (Neale 50% rifle 12 noon 36 per number) at 12 noon Tents (×5) Orders received to move at 2.30 p.m. to new camp area. Tents pitched by Coy. Lit very good, good watering for animals. Baking for men. Site F. 3/4 Mile N of Q in PROVEN. Ordered to have G.S. Ragon Driver + a leader kept attached to Padre to have G.S. Wagon Drivers. No 4 Coy A.S.C. Rum Issues. Handed by Padre Brownegate. Dundee Diaries.	4 R.I.E. Brown 5A. Racoon 5A. Pacoon

Vol 2

Confidential

War Diary

of

221 Coy. Machine Gun Corps

From Aug. 1st 1917   To Aug. 31st 1917

(Volume II.)

Army Form C. 2118.

WAR DIARY
or
INTELLIGENCE SUMMARY.
(Erase heading not required.)

Place	Date	Hour	Summary of Events and Information	Remarks and references to Appendices
PROVEN	1/8/17		Parade all day. Proposed. Message received from O.C. No 1 Section at HARDINGE. Water works all correct.	Map Ref HAZEBROUCK 5.A. 1:100,000
PROVEN	2/8/17		No 1 Section visited by O.C. Company. Parade all day. No work possible. 2 Riding Horses received to complete Estt.	
PROVEN	3/8/17		Company parade. Second to visited No. 1 Section at HARDINGE with pay & rations. Parade all day. No parades possible.	
PROVEN	4/8/17		Conference with D.M.G.O. at 10.30 am. 29th Div. relieving GUARDS Div. Subject:- Preliminary Relief Orders. Reported arrangements for defence & attack. Probable barrage orders. Parade all day. 128 all ranks reported for outpost courses.	
PROVEN	5/8/17		Church Parade 3 p.m. Divisional Relief Orders received 6 p.m. & attached men reported for outly or courses. Total 32 Attached.	C. Coy

WAR DIARY
or
INTELLIGENCE SUMMARY

Army Form C. 2118.

(Erase heading not required.)

Place	Date	Hour	Summary of Events and Information	Remarks and references to Appendices
PROVEN	6/8/17		Getting ready for move	
PROVEN → FIELD	7/8/17	1.45 p.m.	Camp cleared. Left 1.45 pm. Advanced party with Col Wagon left 9 pm. Arrived Camp 14 FOREST AREA via Route "B". Fixed down own bivouacs. Shelters, tents for officers 7.30 pm.	
FIELD	8/8/17		Day spent in extending & improving accommodation. Inspecting. D.A.Q.O gave instruction for arranging with O.C's 87, 96 Bys & Bing up S.A.A.	
"	9/8/17		O.C. 88 Cay & 2 i/c 22y Cay rode up & on return 2/Lay sent up 10,000 rounds & 22y Cay 6,000 rounded S.A.A. I made forward dump at LAPIN TRENCH LANGEMARCK MAP 1/10,000. O/C No.1 Section reported at same time & O.C 87 Coy & took round position to be occupied by Section which was to be attached for barrage fire for next attack. Hull Barrage orders received 3 a.m. 10/8/17.	C.C. ReP.

Army Form C. 2118.

WAR DIARY
or
INTELLIGENCE SUMMARY.
(Erase heading not required.)

Place	Date	Hour	Summary of Events and Information	Remarks and references to Appendices
FIELD	10/8/17		+ Coogh. Barrage Orders for to-days attack received from D. Inf. O. and communicated to Coy Officers. No. 1 Section attached to 87 Inf. Bg. went up at night. Section Officers 234th Section also went Reconnectory Jarm.	
	11/8/17		Barrage orders amendments received. Fatigue parties preparing the barrage position went up to that at night. Report received from O.C. No 1 Sec. on progress of work. O.C. 86 Coy asked for man & Dollow his team in the live for a long period.	
	12/8/17		Further amendments received to Barrage orders also request for reliefs team for 86 Inf. Coy. Sec. up at 4pm. Fatigue parties on Barrage positions went up 4pm. also two days rations for O.C. No 1 Section. Church Parade 3pm.	

WAR DIARY
or
INTELLIGENCE SUMMARY

Army Form C. 2118.

Place	Date	Hour	Summary of Events and Information	Remarks and references to Appendices
Field	13/8/17		Further Barrage Orders amendments issued. C.O. visited Bn Ration in line at night. SAULES FM. selected as Bgde. Battle H.Qs.	
Field	14/8/17		Nos. 2, 3, & 4 Sections took up their barrage positions. Officers & men of 2 & 3 Sections attached to 86 M.G. Coy. formed Harassing Fire & very gun Barrage Orders with sketch attached.	Append. I.
Field	15/8/17		Details and Battle H.Q. Section Party took up their place at SAULES Fm. by 10 p.m. O.O. & 2nd Amend SHOKES FM. & C.O. reported to G.O.C. 87 Inf. Bde. Sections in position shown on map. 2 Rumours from Section attached to Coy. T.R. Zero time 4.45a.m 16th received & passed to C.O. & Sections.	c. Map

WAR DIARY or INTELLIGENCE SUMMARY

Army Form C. 2118.

Place	Date	Hour	Summary of Events and Information	Remarks and references to Appendices
Field	16/8/17		All sections except No 2 Section who suffered several casualties from shellfire opened the barrage as per OO No 1. Later map to take over barrage Zone "E" at OO C33. Later on instructor (Lieut Seaton) Major D.B. Richards was ordered to report to OC KOSB 13	LANGEMARK 1:10,000
			PASSERELLE F.M.U.21.C.30.9.5. Order cancelled during night. Meanwhile owing to Lt. Hunter O.C. No I Section being gassed, relief of "E" Group not completed till following day. Enemy reported massing at U16 A.d. B. Barrage Guns stood By.	
			Orders received. Defence as follows:- Forward Area 12 guns. 88 M.G. Coy Barrage Guns 16 Guns. 23/7 Coy. M.G.C. Casualties 2 Sgts. 1 Cpl. 1 L/Cpl. & 3 men & 1 Officer	
Field	17.8.17		Orders received to take over forward defence from O.C. 88 Coy with 3 sections right 18/19 & hand over barrage positions to O.C. 86 Coy. - Guns tripods spare parts & ammunition to be handed over. O.C. 88 Coy came to fix up relief with C.O.	
Field	18/8/17		S.O.'s orders to report 9.a.m. at H.Q. 18.8.17. Casualties 2 men wounded Section Officers reported at H.Q. for relief orders. C.O. ordered to report to G.O.C. 86th Bde de nouveau. Guns for left forward sector C.O. said his orders usually came C.O. 19 Coy

Army Form C. 2118.

WAR DIARY
or
INTELLIGENCE SUMMARY.
(Erase heading not required.)

Instructions regarding War Diaries and Intelligence Summaries are contained in F. S. Regs., Part II. and the Staff Manual respectively. Title pages will be prepared in manuscript.

Place	Date	Hour	Summary of Events and Information	Remarks and references to Appendices
Field	18/7		Through O.M.G.O till these orders came, he was meanwhile instructed to report to O.C. 16th Middlesex. O.I/c Left Sector regarding positions of this guns. Then sent O.C. 88 M.G.Coy at TUFFS F.M. He guides O.C. No.4 Section ordered to take over guns in present position between V.16.6.6.4. to V.16.6.4.5. + then get into touch with O.C. Middlesex & move guns to positions he wished. Relief complete by 11 p.m. Positions shown on map as follows:-	LANGE MARCK 1:10,000
			No.1 Section	
			U.23. a.1.5	
			U.22. 10.4.5.9.5	
			U.22. 6.8.4	
			U.22. 6.6.4	
			U.22. 6.6.4 Section H.Q.	
			No.3 Section	
			U.22. B.5.9	
			U.22. B.5.4	
			U.22. 6.4.6	
			U.22. a.5.9	
			U.22. 6.6.4 Section H.Q.	
			No.4 Section	
			4 guns between U.16.6.6.4 & U.16.6.4.5.	
			Section H.Q. V.16.6.4.5.	
			Casualties:- nil	
Field	19/7		Moved Coy. H.Q. to SENTIER F.M. with a wire to forward Bde. H.Q. No.4 Section reported unable to get into touch with O.C. Infantry & transfer guns to positions requested owing to swamp & heavy shell fire. This section was in front line. O.M.G.O ordered up another 2 guns. Arranged with 86 Coy for 2 guns to be handed over & teams brought up under Lt Kinahan's C.O.Y. from No.2 Section back in rest to take up positions on left flank. Section H.Q. V.15.6.7.5. Section H.Q. V.15.6.7. + U.15.10.2.7. + U.15.6.8.5.4.5. reported in position 10.30 p.m. at V.15.	

A5834 Wt. W4973/M687 750,000 8.16 D. D. & L. Ltd. Form/C.2113/13

Army Form C. 2118.

WAR DIARY
or
INTELLIGENCE SUMMARY.
(Erase heading not required.)

Instructions regarding War Diaries and Intelligence Summaries are contained in F.S. Regs., Part II and the Staff Manual respectively. Title pages will be prepared in manuscript.

Place	Date	Hour	Summary of Events and Information	Remarks and references to Appendices
Field	14/8/17		At same time O.C. no 4 Section ordered to withdraw 2 guns to Coy H.Q. Ration arrangements in future will be through Coy H.Q. owing to ration parties getting lost at other rendez-vous. Casualties 1 Sgt. 2 men wounded.	
	20/8/17		O.C. Left Section took over 2 guns withdrawn from no 4 Section, & they took up their positions at V.15.6.85.35. During night 20th/21st Orders received that Coy would be relieved by 87 Coy. Guns, Tripods, Spare parts to be handed over. O.C. 87 Coy came to make arrangements about 2 p.m. Relief mans to Section Officers. Casualties 1 Killed 2 men wounded	
	21/8/17		Visited by O.C. M.G.O. in morning. O.C. 87. came up early in afternoon. All but 2 guns in V.16.66.4 & 4.5 relieved. Guides missed relieving sections these 2 guns had to remain till following night. Relief during day impossible. Remaining teams reported to C.O. at FOREST CAMP up to 8 p.m. 21/8. Casualties 1 Sgt 1 man wounded.	
	20/8/17		From O.C. 227 M.C. Coy. to S.O. no --- 3 section FORAGE will relieve FICKLE to-morrow night 21/22. a. Arrange to have all guns, Tripods, ammn. etc ready for handing over & proper receipts taken. Guides for teams will be at Section H.Q. These guides will meet the relieving gun teams on arrival. The runners now with H.Q. will take relieving Section to Section H.Q. a.a. Carry 1 days rations as follows to-night No 1 & 3 Sections to TUFFS. F.M. No 4 Section to KNUSTERS F.M. Left Section Coy. H.Q.	

Army Form C. 2118.

WAR DIARY
or
INTELLIGENCE SUMMARY.
(Erase heading not required.)

Instructions regarding War Diaries and Intelligence Summaries are contained in F. S. Regs., Part II. and the Staff Manual respectively. Title pages will be prepared in manuscript.

Place	Date	Hour	Summary of Events and Information	Remarks and references to Appendices
Field	20/8/17		Detailed receipts must be obtained for every-thing handed over. If any trench stores have been taken these will be included. On being relieved the Sections will move off independently & report to O.C. Coy. on arrival at Forrest Camp.	
			Omitted from 20/8/17	
	22/8/17		Received message from O.C. 87 Coy. & O.C. 2 Guns to say relief not carried out. Sections Recd'd. Coy Strength 9 Officers 163 O.R. excluding Sections Casualties nil. Attached.	
	23/8/17		2 Gun teams were relieved night 21/22 and returned Coys 9.30am the arrangement for exchange of equipment guns Lewis gun & ammunition has caused much difficulty. First Coys were fully equipped on getting here & take over ammunition of equipment. In future no complete Lewis R had over Bipods & ammunition only takes and gun jumpers & other equipment. Actions cleaned up & located Reinforcements — Lt Bryot 9 Other Ranks Orders received to relieve to left guns — Lewis guns from 87h S.S. Bn Coy C Coy St Barthelemy & O.C. arranged	

A 5834 Wt. W4973/M587, 750,000 8/16 D. D. & L. Ltd. Forms/C.2115/13.

Army Form C. 2118.

WAR DIARY
or
INTELLIGENCE SUMMARY.
(Erase heading not required.)

Place	Date	Hour	Summary of Events and Information	Remarks and references to Appendices
Area	24/8/17		9 Other Ranks reported from In G Base Depot. L. Marshaw + 8 O.R. relieved & took over 4 guns of 87 Coy. in vicinity of MONTMIRAIL tm. for any tell night 27/28	
	25/8/17		Orders received to hand over Camp & to Guards In O.C. & take over Partridge Camp N 26.C.05 PROVEN AREA. Took over part of guns & Equipment from 87 Coy. Settlement of equipment postponed till all Coys. sick in res.	
	26/8/17		1 Officer & 14 O.R. left to await relief of Lt Mathews & teams. Remainder of transport & Coy. marched off at 11 am. for PARTRIDGE CAMP. Found camp very dirty & clean on arrival. 1 Sgt. & 1 man evacuated being reported sick. Strength Officers 10 O.R. 178 Attached (Canadian)	C.C.P.O.T

A3834 Wt.W4973/M637. 750,000 8/16 D. D. & L. Ltd. Form/C.1113/13.

WAR DIARY
or
INTELLIGENCE SUMMARY.

(Erase heading not required.)

Army Form C. 2118.

Place	Date	Hour	Summary of Events and Information	Remarks and references to Appendices
PROYART	27/6/17		Horse exercise of Section HQ & Learned Horses Lt Stephens team relieves by guards night 27/28.	
"	28/6/17		Reveille 6.30 am. Breakfast 7.45 am. Section Officers Inspection. Inspection of Lines 9 a.m. Squadron left Droyal 10 am. Rain most of day. The training to be started till guns & equipment were complete from other Cos. Lines a fine standing were made.	
"	29/6/17		10 men from 2nd Reinforcement Dismounted Regiment so round 10 attached B.R. from 28th Bage and told to take B.horses for all O.R. Coys & 20 gun gears to be left from 3rd so Coy H.Q. (copy) 10 Officers W O.R. 28 Order.	C.C.Reg.

Army Form C. 2118.

WAR DIARY
or
INTELLIGENCE SUMMARY.
(Erase heading not required.)

Place	Date	Hour	Summary of Events and Information	Remarks and references to Appendices
PROVEN	30/9/17		Routine as usual. Conference of D.A.G.O. & O.C. Coys at 5 p.m. 2 Y.C. Chargers cast.	
	31/9/17		Routine as usual. Exchanges & settling efficiency guns commenced. Strength 10 officers 170 O.R. 18 carts. Animals 6 Riding 47 draulers	

C. C. Pryn

App^x I

COPY.

29th Division M.G. Barrage Instructions

Guns available.

```
227 M.G.Coy. ----------------------------- 16 guns
 87  "   "   less 2 sections. ------------  8 guns.
 88  "   "     "    "    "    ------------  8  "
 86  "   "     "    "    "    ------------  8  "
                                    Total.  40 guns.
```

Distribution.

These guns will be divided into 10 Groups of 4 guns each (A-K) For purposes of preparation and control these will be divided into 3 larger Groups as follows:-

1. Groups A,B,C,D. found by 227 M.G.Coy. under O.C 227 M.G.COY.

2. { " E. ------------ 86 M.G.Coy. } under O.C. 87 " "
     { F,G. ----------- 87 " "   }

3. { " H,I. ----------8 88 " " } under O.C. 88 COY.
     { K. ------------ 86 " " }

These groups will be along the line LOEBECK FARM --MAJORS FM-- --ABRI FM--U 26 Central--U26 d.8.6. with A Group at LOEBECK FM and K Group at U 26 d.8.6.

EMPLACEMENTS.

Pits may be dug or shell holes converted. In either case platform must sandbagged and made firm. Tripod bases are available if required. Limits of traverse and search must be blocked for each gun before Y day.

AMUNITION.

35 Belts per gun will be the average amount fired. Each Barrage gun will be provided with 5 Spare Belts in addition to existing 14 Belts per gun. These will be filled before Zero. 400,000 rounds S.A.A. is being got up to ABRI WOOD and from this, dumps of 40,000 rounds will be made by each group of 4 guns.

WATER.

ONE petrol tin for gun and one for gun-team to be at each gun position before Zero.

Rate of Fire.

ONE Belt in 4 mins. during an advance and one belt in 10 mins. during a pause. Belt-filling arrangements must be made to keep up with this rate as far as possible.

Barrels.

Each Gun will start with a new Barrel. A few rounds should be fired beforehand to remove Grease Packing. Barrels will be changed on completion of Barrage. Not more than one gun in each group to change barrels at a time.

Bearings.

All compasses should be tested and errors noted. Steel Helmets and tripods should not be near enough to effect bearings. As there are few landmarks each group should erect posts at suitable distances for Ref. Objects. Gun positions must be checked by measurement as well as re-section. Range-finding instruments can be used for this.

Danger Space.

Each Group Commander will arrange to mark out the danger space immediately in front of his group and will arrange to warn troops in the neighbourhood. The danger space must not include any regular track or duck-walk that will be required for communication or reinforcements.

DG.9. The following addendum is being issued to instructions no. 9.
1 Communication will be by runner (2) H.Q. will be as follows :- Left Group (227 Coy M.G.C) will be near L. Bde. H.Q SAULES FM U 25. B 22 Centre & Right Groups (87 & 88 M.G Coys) will be at U 26. C 3. 2. One runner per section will be with H.Q. of each of above Groups Left Group will keep in close touch with Left Bde O's. C. above groups will arrange to have one runner with D.M.G.O who will be at WOOD HO C 2. A 2. 7 till Z + 4 hrs. 30. Centre and right groups will keep in close touch with Right Bde.

Vol 3

Confidential

War Diary

of

227 Coy. Machine Gun Corps

from 1-9-1917 to 30-9-1917

(Volume iii.)

From O.C. 227 Coy
           M.G.C.
To D.H.Q.
     29th Division

Herewith original War Diary
for month of Sept 1917 please.

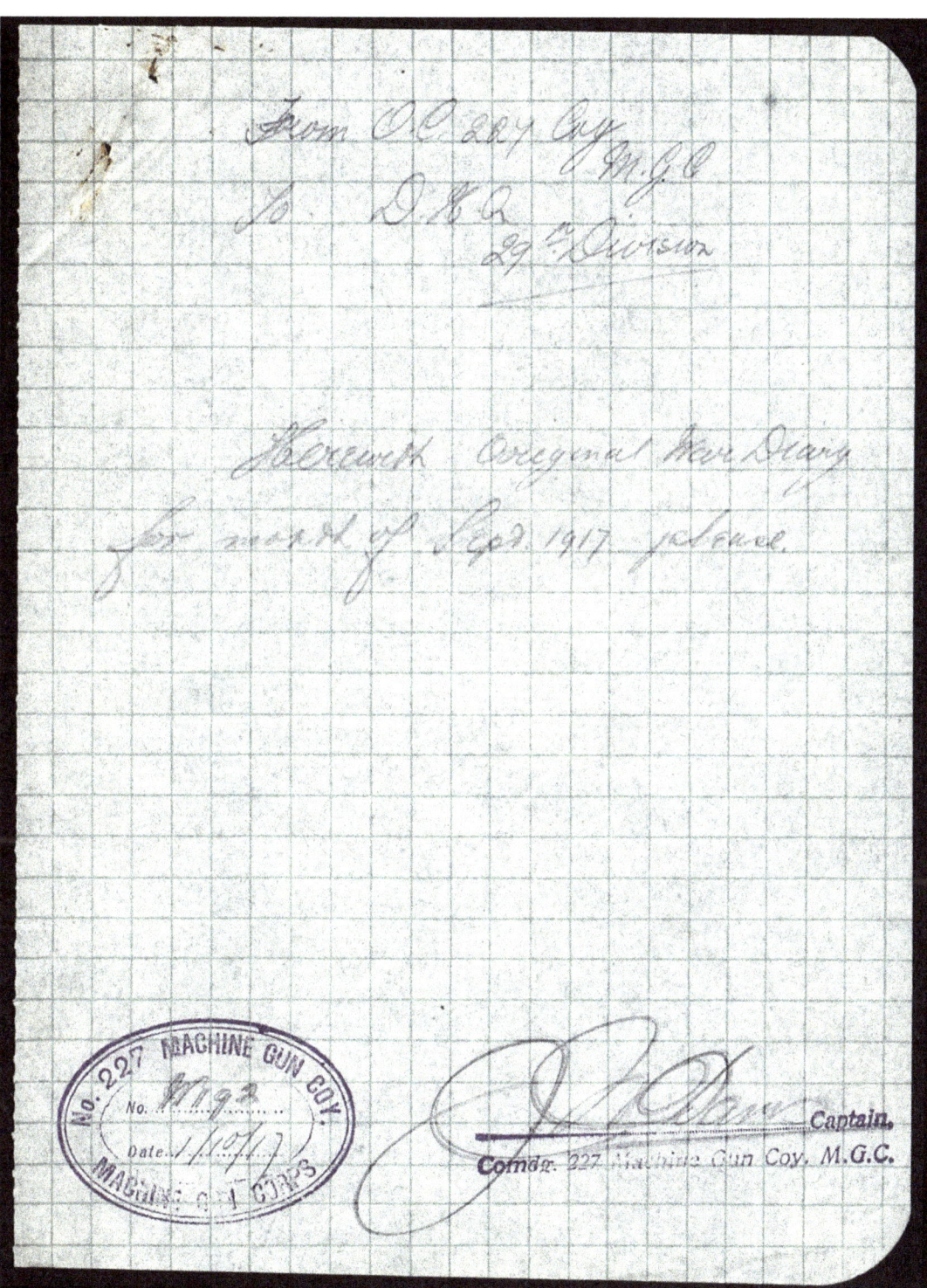

Comdg. 227 Machine Gun Coy. M.G.C.

WAR DIARY
INTELLIGENCE SUMMARY
(Erase heading not required.)

Army Form C. 2118.

Place	Date	Hour	Summary of Events and Information	Remarks and references to Appendices
PROYEN	1/9/17		Orders received re training to commence Monday 2nd. Programme submitted. Coy deficient of spare parts through acting out after conference	
"	2/9/17		Church Parade 11.30 am at Ecole Reg. Lines. Heavily rained during to rain. L.O.s reported from C.R.S.	
"	3/9/17		Parades :- 9-10am P.O.'s Inspection & Infy Drill. 10-10.30am Elementary Gun Drill 10.30-11am Combined Drill. 11-12 noon Immersion Action 12-12.30pm Stripping 2-2.30pm Care & Cleaning 3-4 pm Pickingathers. Fine day. Several visits of hostile aeroplanes by night but no bombing in vicinity.	
"	4/9/17		Parades :- 9-10am L.O.s inspection & S.G. 10-11am Lect Animal Drill or 11-12 noon Lecture by L.O.'s on "Barrage Fire" practice pasting 7 minutes elevation by chronometer & Elevation Dial. 2-3pm Pasting on direction by Compass & R.O. 3-4 pm Company Drill	C. C. Major

WAR DIARY
or
INTELLIGENCE SUMMARY.
(Erase heading not required.)

Army Form C. 2118.

Instructions regarding War Diaries and Intelligence Summaries are contained in F. S. Regs., Part II. and the Staff Manual respectively. Title pages will be prepared in manuscript.

Place	Date	Hour	Summary of Events and Information	Remarks and references to Appendices
PROVEN	4/9/17		1 Sgt joined from Base Depot. Strength:— 10 Officers 103 O.R.	
			Animals 6 Riding horses 47 D. Mules.	
"	5/9/17		Parades:— 9-9.30am Section Officers Inspection	
			11-12 noon Bayonet Fighting	
			9.30-10.00am Coy Drill by C.O.	
			Section parties on duty of Coy 2/c	
			10-11am Combined Drill	
			12-12.30pm Case Cleaning	
			1.30-3pm Baths. Visited by D.A.G.O.	
"	6/9/17		Parades:— 9-9.30am Section Officers Inspection	
			9.30-10am Section Drill.	
			10-11am Rest Animal Drill	
			11-12 noon Instruction & practice	
			12-12.30pm Case Cleaning.	of relief of trenches
"	7/9/17		Parades:— 9-10am L.O's Inspection & Section Drill. 10-11am P.T. 11-12.30pm Bab Fatigues	Capt Cleary
			There was a demonstration of concentration & distribution of Rifle-with & guns	
			firing out the new methods taught at CAMIERS. The demonstration was held	
			& conducted by Lt In G Coy. Knight firing both made from an ammunition cap. & C.O.C.	
			was also seen	

A6943 Wt. W14422/M1160. 350,000. 12/16 D. D. & L. Forms/C/2118/14.

Army Form C. 2118.

WAR DIARY
or
INTELLIGENCE SUMMARY.
(Erase heading not required.)

Instructions regarding War Diaries and Intelligence Summaries are contained in F. S. Regs., Part II. and the Staff Manual respectively. Title pages will be prepared in manuscript.

Place	Date	Hour	Summary of Events and Information	Remarks and references to Appendices
PROVEN	8/9/17		Parades :- 9 - 9.30 P.O. Inspections, Rifles, Ammn. Etc.	
		9.30 - 10 am	P.T.	
		10 - 11 am	Route March, Over Country, over Rough Ground	
		11 - 12 noon	Company Drill	
		12 - 12.30 pm	Coy's Cleaning	
	9/9/17		Church Parade on the Lines by Reverend McClain 11 am	
	10/9/17	9 - 10 am	Cleaning & Dubbing Equipment & L.O.	
		10 - 11 am	Instruction & Practice in Barrage Fire.	
		11 - 12.30 pm	Section Tactical Exercises.	
		3.30 pm	Lecture. Officers, N.C.O's and Aeroplane.	
			All Officers & Lectr. visited aerodrome & watched aeroplane ascension & descension.	
			Lights 100 - 1000, 1600 & 4000.	
	11/9/17	8 - 9.30 am	Dispersion, Inspection Drill 9.30 - 10.30 am P.T.	
		10.30 - 11.30	Practice on Barrage Fire by L.O's 11.30 - 12.30 Combined Drill	
			Strength 10 Officers 120 O.R. L.P.R. a7 Lectr.	e.c P.Cox

A6945 Wt. W11422/M160 350,000 12/16 D.D. & L. Forms/C/2118/14.

WAR DIARY
or
INTELLIGENCE SUMMARY.
(Erase heading not required.)

Army Form C. 2118.

Instructions regarding War Diaries and Intelligence Summaries are contained in F. S. Regs., Part II. and the Staff Manual respectively. Title pages will be prepared in manuscript.

Place	Date	Hour	Summary of Events and Information	Remarks and references to Appendices
PROVEN	12/9/17		Parades:— 9-10am Combined Drill. 10-11am /Cavalry Group of Drill. 11-12noon Lecture.	
			Auction with Concentration & Distribution fire with S.C.O. 12-12.30 Cavalry	
"	13/9/17		Baths 9am. Parades:— 9-10am L.O. inspection of Section Drill. 10-11am practice	
			for Concentration & Distribution Fire Drill. 12.12.30 Gas Chamber	
"	14/9/17		Range Distance 25 yards, sighted to the Coy. 13.14.15.16. 1 & 2 Letters 9-11.	
			3rd Sections 11-1pm. Sr. & Jr. officers carried out Practices over their own	
			arrangements. Football in afternoon. 2/Lts. Ivenham + L/Cpl. Barings	
			Proceeded to L.O. Course at St. Omer.	
"	15/9/17		Range 9am - 11am.	
"	16/9/17		Church Parade 11am in Divisional Theatre PROVEN.	
			Non-conformists 9.15am at 8th Field Amb. R.E. 10am PROVEN	
"	17/9/17		Parades:— 9-10am L.O.s inspection & Section Drill. 10-11am Barrage Drill	
			11-12.30pm Section tactical Exercise.	
"	18/9/17		Parades:— 9-10am L.O.s Inspection & Section Drill. 10-11am P.T. 11-12.30pm open Barrage	D. Cpt.
			Drill in preparation for Barrage Equipment for 1st Line.	C
			I.R.O.O. returned from Gas Course	

Army Form C. 2118.

WAR DIARY
or
INTELLIGENCE SUMMARY.
(Erase heading not required.)

Instructions regarding War Diaries and Intelligence Summaries are contained in F.S. Regs., Part II and the Staff Manual respectively. Title pages will be prepared in manuscript.

Place	Date	Hour	Summary of Events and Information	Remarks and references to Appendices
PROYEN	19/9/17		Parades:- 9-10am S.O. Inspection & Section Drill 10-11am Combined Drill	
			11-12 noon Barrage Drill 12-12.30pm Cable Closing	
			3 P.M. O. & 2 men returned from Telephone Course.	
PROYEN	20/9/17		Parades:- 9-10am S.O. Inspection & Section Drill 10-11am Combined Drill	
			10-11 noon Barrage Drill 12-12.30pm Cable Closing	
			Administrative Orders No 17 & 24 Div Order No 134 received with amendments	App. I.
			attached. By B & Colws & Cos H.Q. & Cy Liaison Centres to Lines H.Q. & 2	
			Sections in Horses Area. Cy Officer arrived.	
	21/9/17		Sections & Transport under I.O. packed by advance party	
			moved off at half hour intervals commencing at 9am. Col	Map Ref: LANGEMARCK 1.10,000
			arrived Cp 12.30pm Found Camp much improved by Canaders	
FIELD	22/9/17		Nos 1 & 2 Sections took over positions from 2 sections at MIDTENDRIFT. Commanding	
			SIGNAL Fan Section moved 2.30pm & Transport 4.30pm Commanding	
			Officer & Major M.F.R. proceeded up with Transport to spend night with	
			No1 Section at MAP. for all positions & interview G.O.C. 75th Bde C	
			& Bn G.O. visited Camp at 5.10pm & wished to meet C.O. at	C

A6945 Wt. W14421/M1160 350,000. 12/16 D.D. & L. Forms/C./2118/14.

Army Form C. 2118.

WAR DIARY
or
INTELLIGENCE SUMMARY.
(Erase heading not required.)

Instructions regarding War Diaries and Intelligence Summaries are contained in F. S. Regs., Part II. and the Staff Manual respectively. Title pages will be prepared in manuscript.

Place	Date	Hour	Summary of Events and Information	Remarks and references to Appendices
				Map ref BROEN BEEK 1/10,000
FIELD	23/9/17		VULCAN CROSSING at 6.45 a.m. 23rd. to reconnoitre positions under Div area with D.B.G.O. 20th Div. Message sent up Strength O.R. O.R. 181	
			C.O. accompanied D.B.G.O. 20th & 29th Divs. to reconnoitre positions owing to 29th probably taking over 20th Div. front. Church parades at FOREST AREA of C/G 18. 90th Lewton gave demonstration of Brigade through B.C. & B.G. Coy + Coy O.C. U16 a95 and U16 b67. Cheerwood 3 letters per gan 12 letter || Casualties O.R. 1 killed 2 wounded. 1 attached wounded Strength – O.R. O.R. 178 O.R. OR 25	
"	24/9/17		C.O. proceeded by Car with D.B.G.O. & O.C. 86 Coy & Cameron to see demonstration of M.G. Barrage fire. 2 to write he 1.2 letter on the line. All going well. No. 1 Section at SIGNAL FARM ordered to open indirect fire 11-40 a.m. — 11-50 a.m. on U16 a 95. U16 b 67 by 18th Brigade through O.C. 86 In G Coy enemy retrose bombard Hey area. 3 letter bn. gun — 12 letter	
"	25/9/17		O.C. Coy ordered to bring fire on U17 a 59 & U10 d 7203 T between U10 d 03 & U16 f 690 at Zero time on 26th Sep. Battin	C O

A6945 Wt. W14422/M1160 350,000 12/16 D. D. & L. Forms/C/2118/14.

Army Form C. 2118.

WAR DIARY
or
INTELLIGENCE SUMMARY
(Erase heading not required.)

Place	Date	Hour	Summary of Events and Information	Remarks and references to Appendices
			went up to act with the [?] on these targets. C.O. more H.Q. at SIGNAL Fm. fortnight 25/26. The barrage were in conjunction with attack of Corps on right.	
FIELD	26/9/17		Fire opened at 5.50 a.m. & continued at rate of 1 b.o. per gun per 10 mins = x-1+95. 1 b.o. per gun per hour x+95-x time was 9.30 a.m. Ammunition expended 19,000 rounds Shelling caused much damage in charge of position or in countation of positions. No casualties were suffered by this gun 10. TOR up for Hr. Burn	
"	27/9/17		C.O. returned to No 3 Section. O.C. on Section at WIDENDRIFT suffered 3 more casualties. Relieved at night by this subsection officer & O.R. O.R. Strength – 10 O. 170 O.R. to M.S.L.D 4 P.H. O.R. 24 + 60. O.R. 80 34+1 Letters were 2 up to line Barrage position	
	28/9/17		for Nos 1, 3 & 4 Section were recommitted down STEENBEEK. D.S.C. made arrangements never cunning of D.B.C.O. for making S.A.R. dump at DERAIN For, ammunition to be brought up by light Railway from PABRI DUMP. Work to commence on 29th.	P.Chr C 1

A6945 Wt.W11422/M1160 350,000 12/16 D. D. & L. Forms/C/2118/14.

Army Form C. 2118.

WAR DIARY
or
INTELLIGENCE SUMMARY.
(Erase heading not required.)

Instructions regarding War Diaries and Intelligence Summaries are contained in F. S. Regs., Part II. and the Staff Manual respectively. Title pages will be prepared in manuscript.

Place	Date	Hour	Summary of Events and Information	Remarks and references to Appendices
Field.	29/9/17		Nos. 1 & 2 Sections relieved by Nos. 3 & 4 Sections. 2 Lewis carriers in No. 3. Fatigue party under 2/Lt. Hackson toth cages S.A.A. & Light line to DENAIN Fm. & commenced L.O.A. M.G. Dumps. One sick evacuated	
"	30/9/17		Work on barrage position in progress. 3 O.P.'s in Coy from Bois. Operation & Barrage Orders received from Div. Details Appdx:— O.1.O. O.O. 171. Appendices last month	c DCu/r c

APPENDIX
I
COPY

Company Orders
by
Captain J. W. Davis
Cdng 227 M.G. Coy

Field   20-9-17

Duties Officers for duty to-morrow 2/Lt. J. Wadham
           Next for duty 2/Lt A.J Bridgeman

Move The Coy will relieve 4th Gds
      M G Coy at FOREST AREA on
morning 21st
        Reveille _ _ _ _ _   6.30 a.m
        Breakfasts _ _ _ _ _   7 a.m.
Ado Party with G.S. Wagon
        Move off _ _ _ _ _   9 a.m.
Transport with limbers
Cookers move off   10 a.m.
No 1 Section _ _ _ _ _   9.45 a.m.

No 2 Section _ _ _ _ _   10.15 a.m.

No 3 Section _ _ _ _ _   10.45 a.m.

No 4 Section _ _ _ _ _   11 a.m.

These times will be strictly

adhered to.

Route   P+ Area X Roads - 27/F1c20g
 — BELGIAN CHEMIN MILITAIRE
 - Road Junc. 28/A 2 b q 5.30
 - Road Junc. 20/S 27 a 2 0.
 - Road Junc. 20/S 28 d q 2
DE WIPPE CABARET.

C C Bamber Capt
for O.C. 227 M.G. Coy.

Vol 4

Confidential

War Diary
of
227 Coy. Machine Gun Corps

from 1/10/1917 to 31/10/1917

(Volume IV.)

From:- O.C 227 Coy
           M.G.C.
To:- D.H.Q
         29th Division

Herewith original War Diary
for month of October 1917.

Captain,
Comdg. 227 Machine Gun Coy. M.G.C.

WAR DIARY
or
INTELLIGENCE SUMMARY.
(Erase heading not required.)

Army Form C. 2118.

Place	Date	Hour	Summary of Events and Information	Remarks and references to Appendices
FIELD	1/10/17		Barrage & operation orders appeared. Gunposition & targets as shown on tracing. Orders sent to O.C. Batteries line O.C. No. 4 Section instructed to reconnoitre U27 C 45.30 – U.27 C 65.05 so as to bring fire to bear along line of railway in case of right flank going away. One gun of No.3 Section at WIJDENDRIFT moved under orders of O.C. Left Group to U.21 a.75.40 giving excellent field of fire & strong enemy infantry line. Animals & Gun Park inspected by D.D.V.S. Report 29th ult received through Division Exact of report 29th. Div. No. 268/5/11 " Animals looking very well & well groomed, strong food. Barrage arrangements of each Section nearly complete. Winter camp commenced. Transport officer engaged in erecting covered mule standings.	
FIELD	2/10/17		Further instructions & emendments to barrage orders received. C.O. endeavoured to personally check Gun positions. Barrage Running, pegs & compasses, no barrage of any Section as in enfilade. L/Cpl Clutterbuck does very good work as draughtsman in the	

WAR DIARY
or
INTELLIGENCE SUMMARY.
(Erase heading not required.)

Army Form C. 2118.

Place	Date	Hour	Summary of Events and Information	Remarks and references to Appendices
			evening a fatigue party under 2/Lt Haslam took 10000 rounds S.A.A. to DENAIN Fm by light railway from Abn tool dump. No 3 Section found an old German trench near their position which accommodated their four guns. Strength O. 10 OR. 176 Medical OR. 28	
FIELD	3/10/17		C.O. moved up line and made his H.Q. at Signal farm. All barrage positions completed by 7 pm. CO personally checked direction of guns. By 8 pm all barrage guns received Zero time which was 6.0 am following morning. Reinforcements of gunners joined Coy from Base Depot. Strength O 10 OR.177 Medical	
	4/10/17		Barrage opened at 6.0 am on enemy. Nos 1 + 4 Sections were subjected to heavy shelling. This became more intense at the attack on the right returned. Casualties. No 1 Section 1 NCO wounded No 3 Section 1 NCO + 1 OR killed, 1 OR wounded. Officer 1 OR killed. 2 OR wounded. No 4 Section 1 OR killed + 1 OR wounded. On the evening No 3 Section was relieved from Widgerdrift Lm by No 2 Section. In the evening No 1 Section were relieved by O.M.G.O. to withdraw their guns +	

Army Form C. 2118.

WAR DIARY
or
INTELLIGENCE SUMMARY.
(Erase heading not required.)

Instructions regarding War Diaries and Intelligence Summaries are contained in F. S. Regs., Part II. and the Staff Manual respectively. Title pages will be prepared in manuscript.

Place	Date	Hour	Summary of Events and Information	Remarks and references to Appendices
	3/10/17		Take up old Barrage positions at Signal Farm. Casualties 2nd Lt /c Wounded Lt. R. J. Matthews took over duties of 2nd Lt /c. Strength Officers 8. O.R. 172. Attached O.R. 27.	
	5/10/17		Early in morning O.C. no 1 Section received orders from Lt.Col G.O. to reconnoitre positions for Hyperion 6" Guns for a tactical offensive scheme in Langemarck O.C. no 2 Section details its places its Guns as follows :- 1 Gun Rat Nest Farm, 1/ Augment Station - 2 Martins White. White Guns were in position by dusk. This scheme was subsequent to O.C. the C.O. and no 1 sect. Lts appeared in the evening no 3 & 4 Sections were re-emplaced by the 4th eds. M & G coy from Chez Fourier at Wild Wood site & Signal Farm. The Sections returned to Camp about 9.p.m. Advance party moved to ELVERDINGE at 5 p.m. & took over the huts at WHITE MILL Camp. Huts very clean & airy. Strength Officers 8. O.R. 172. Attached O.R. 27.	
	6/10/17		Remainder of Coy moved to WHITE MILL Camp with limbers etc. Limbers left at Camp & Mules returned to horse lines BARCLAY WOOD. Details for L.G.S. etc. as follows :- Transport Lines BARCLAY WOOD. Details to M.E. Barrage on Oct 9th Reviewed. 19th L.G. Order no 6. G.S. O.I.E. as follows :- Barrage Guns to be divided into 3 Groups viz A. Section 227 & 6 Lys on Platoon.	

Army Form C. 2118.

WAR DIARY
or
INTELLIGENCE SUMMARY.
(Erase heading not required.)

Place	Date	Hour	Summary of Events and Information	Remarks and references to Appendices
	6/10/17		Group B (1 section of 227 M.G. Coy, 1 Section of 88 M.G. Coy) about V.23.a.6.	
			Group C (1 " " 227, -"-, 1 " " 86 -"-) V.23.a.6.3.	
			On completion of Barrage Groups B & C will move forward to general line North	
			Bank of BROEMBEEK in V.17.B & V.18.A. Group to will not move forward	
			until Group B is reported in position.	
			– Barrage Table –	
			Group No. of Barrage ZERO TIME TARGET	
			A 1 0 – 0.4 NAMUR CROSSING	
			2 guns 227 Coy 2 0.4 – 0.16 NAMUR CROSSING – 44K	
			FORTRES FARM 3 0.16 – 0.20 44 K to Extreme Range	
			B	
			4 guns 88 Coy 4 0.20 – 0.40 V.12.6.9.8 – V.12.D.5.4	
			4 " 227 Coy 5 0.40 – 1.50 CAIRO Ho – V.12.d.65.95	
			V.23.a.1.6 6 1.50 – 2.30 V.1.c.o.o – V.7.a.5.6.	

Army Form C. 2118.

WAR DIARY
or
INTELLIGENCE SUMMARY.
(Erase heading not required.)

Place	Date	Hour	Summary of Events and Information	Remarks and references to Appendices
	6.10.17		Group w of Barrage Zero Time Target.	
			10	
			4 gms 9 & 6 by 4 0.20 - 0.40 V12.d.7.5 - V7.c.2.0	
			4. - 127. 5 0.40 - 1.50 TAUBE.F.M - V7.Ø.7.9.	
			V.23.a.6.3 6 1.50 - 2.30	
			Rate of fire will be 1 belt in 10 minutes, except at the following times, when 1 belt in 4 minutes will be fired - 0 to 0.20, 1.46 to 1.50, 2.26 to 2.30.	
			In the evening the Barrage positions were reconnoitred. Strength Off. 6. O.R. 172. Attached 27/men.	
	7/10/17		Church Parade 9.a.m at ELVERDINGHE CHATEAU.	
			Under direction of C.O. 10,000 Rds. S.A.A. were dumped at ABRI WooD by transport along with 4 guns etc for Groups B + C. Group A Guns already in position. A Fatigue party under Capt. Wadham then took it by light railway and dumped it at MARTINS MILL	
			In the evening the Sections of this Coy. No.1 Section under 2/Lt Pryor in B Group & No.2 Section under 2/Lt Kinahan in C. Groups were taken to their respective positions	
			preparatory to digging barrage positions. Casualties 1 O.R. attached sick, evacuated	
			Strength Officers 8. O.R. 172. Attached O.R. 96.	

Army Form C. 2118.

WAR DIARY
or
INTELLIGENCE SUMMARY.
(Erase heading not required.)

Place	Date	Hour	Summary of Events and Information	Remarks and references to Appendices
	8/10/17		At 2 a.m. these sections dug their barrage positions. In the evening emplacements were completed & guns mounted & everything was ready for barrage. By 7 p.m. all barrage groups informed of Z ero hour which was 5.20 a.m. on 9 ᵗʰ. Strength Officers 8 O.R. 172 Attached O.R. 26.	
	9/10/17		At 5.20 a.m. A Group opened fire on given targets, and fired for 20 minutes. These four guns fired smoothly, & in accordance with barrage orders. The two right hand positions were heavily shelled, but apparently without observation of barrage. These guns were taken to previous tactical positions on completion of barrage. At 5.40 a.m. B & C Groups opened fire on their respective targets, and continued firing until Z + 2.30. On completion of this barrage these two groups moved forward. B Group under orders of 188 Coy M.G.C. to V.17. D.5.2. & C Group under orders of this Company to positions at V.18. C.4.5. These two Groups at once prepared new barrage positions & ran S.O.S. Barrage extending from V.1.Q.5.1 - Jurenne crossing to Ste W.8.a.8.4. B. Group taking left sector & C. Group the right sector. At 1 p.m. A Group mounted 2 guns at REITRES F.M & MARTINS MILL for Anti-Aircraft work. At 5.30 p.m. A Group returned to WHITE MILL Camp ELVERDINGHE.	

WAR DIARY or INTELLIGENCE SUMMARY

Army Form C. 2118.

Place	Date	Hour	Summary of Events and Information	Remarks and references to Appendices
	9/10/17		Strength Officers 8. O.R. 172. Attached O.R. 26	
	10/10/17		Early in morning rations were brought up on pack mules to Langemarck Station. At 8.10 a.m. orders were received from 10 M.G.O. that the two sections holding Barrage Positions would be relieved. Guides were at BOESINGHE at 1 p.m. to bring up 2.36 M.G. Coy for relief. By 5.30 p.m. relief was complete, and Gun Equipment was carried to VULCAN CROSSING, where limbers were waiting. Everybody was in WHITE MILL CAMP by 9.00 p.m. Orders rec. move to Proven area received. Two Officers taken on Strength. One Reported. Strength Officers 10. O.R. 172. Attached. O.R. 26	
	11/10/17		og 9 Div Order no 162 Coy 22 received Advanced Party moved to PROVEN. Coy entrained at ELVERDINGHE at 5 a.m. for POMPEY CAMP PROVEN area. Map Ref. Sheet 27 E.12. D.3.8. Transport moved by road at 9 a.m. This camp was taken over in good condition. One man reported from hospital. Coy Rested for remainder of day. Strength Officers 10. O.R. 173. Attached O.R. 26	
	12/10/17		9.a.m. Inspection by section officers. 9.30 - 12.15. Sorting out equipment & cleaning guns. The M.C.O. left for RFC H.Q. with a view to being transferred to England for a Commission.	

A6945 Wt. W11422/M1166 350,000 12/16 D.D. & L. Forms/C, 2118/14.

Army Form C. 2118.

WAR DIARY
or
INTELLIGENCE SUMMARY.
(Erase heading not required.)

Instructions regarding War Diaries and Intelligence Summaries are contained in F. S. Regs., Par. II. and the Staff Manual respectively. Title pages will be prepared in manuscript.

Place	Date	Hour	Summary of Events and Information	Remarks and references to Appendices
	12/4/17		Strength Officers 10 O.R. 172 Attached O.R. 26	
	13/4/17		Parades 9 am. Inspection by SOs 9.30 & 12.15 pm at disposal of S.O. Received Out Order to C.O.S. 6.5 pm warning order for move	
	14/4/17		Strength Officers 10 O.R. 172 Attached O.R. 26 Parades:- 8.50 am Coy & Parade for Divine Service at Church Army Hut at PROVEN. 9.30 am R.C. Parade for Divine Service	
	15/4/17		Strength Officers 10 O.R. 172 Attached O.R. 26 Parades 9 am Inspection by SOs 9.30 & 12.30 pm at S.Os disposal. Movement Order received 11.30 am. Coy left POPPERINGHE Camp at 3.50 pm and entrained at PESELHOEK at 9.30 p.m for HENDECOURT. Strength:- Officers 9 O.R. 172 Attached O.R. 26. 1 Officer adm Hospital earlier returned off strength.	
	16/4/17		Company arrived SAULTY Railhead at 1.40 pm. Company Limbers delivered by Coy of Y.O.L.B. Coy 6/5 SAULTY to 2 pm and marched via BEAUMETZ & RANSART to HENDECOURT, arriving 7.30 p.m. Camp at X 17 h 9.8 taken over for clean course	

A6945 Wt. W14422/M1160 350,000 12/16 D. D. & L. Forms/C./2118/14.

Army Form C. 2118.

WAR DIARY
or
INTELLIGENCE SUMMARY.
(Erase heading not required.)

Instructions regarding War Diaries and Intelligence Summaries are contained in F. S. Regs., Part II. and the Staff Manual respectively. Title pages will be prepared in manuscript.

Place	Date	Hour	Summary of Events and Information	Remarks and references to Appendices
FIELD	17/10/17		Strength :- Officers 9 O.R. 172 Attached O.R. 26.	
			Parades 9am S.O.s Inspection 9.30am – 12.15pm Cleaning Limbers	
			& the Greys engaged in burying stables	
	18/10/17		Strength :- Officers 9 O.R. 172 Attached O.R. 26.	
			Parades 9am S.O.s Inspection 9.30am – 12.30pm Cleaning & Packing Limbers	
			2 Cpls left for R.E. Base for transfer to England for Gas Course of Instruction	
	19/10/17		Strength :- Officers 9 O.R. 170 Attached O.R. 26.	
			Parades 9am S.O.s Inspection 9.30 – 10.30 Checking Gun Equipment	
	20/10/17		Strength :- Officers 9 O.R. 170 Attached O.R. 26.	
			Parades 9am S.O.s Inspection 9.30 – 11.30 Route March.	
	21/10/17		Strength :- Officers 9 O.R. 170 Attached O.R. 26.	
			C of E Parade for Divine Service with Middlesex Regt at 11.15 am	
			R.C. & Non Conformists Parade at 9.30am	
			Three O.R. Transferred to 88th M.G. Coy. 1 O.R. Evacuated.	
			Strength :- Officers 9 O.R. 166 Attached O.R. 26.	

Army Form C. 2118.

WAR DIARY
or
INTELLIGENCE SUMMARY.
(Erase heading not required.)

Instructions regarding War Diaries and Intelligence Summaries are contained in F. S. Regs., Part II. and the Staff Manual respectively. Title pages will be prepared in manuscript.

Place	Date	Hour	Summary of Events and Information	Remarks and references to Appendices
Field	22/10/17		Parades:- 9- 9.30am S.O's Inspection. 9.30-10.30 Squad Drill 10.30-11.45 Platoon Gun Drill 11.45-12.15pm Arms Cleaning. Strength O9. O.R 116. October O.R 26.	
	23/10/17		Parades:- 9-9.30 S.O's Inspection 9.30-10.30 Company Drill 10.45-11.45 Bayonet Drill 11.45-12.15 Arms Cleaning. Strength O9. O.R 115. I.O.R evacuated (sick)	
	24/10/17		Parades:- 9- 9.30am Inspection by O.C. 9.30-10.30 Squad Drill 10.45-11.45 Rapid Service Drill 1.30 p.m Coy paraded for Bath	
	25/10/17		Parades:- 9- 9.30 S.O's Inspection 9.30-10.30 Bayonet Drill 10.45-11.45 Barrage Drill 11.45-12.15 Arms Cleaning. Strength O9. O.R 114. 4 O.R evacuated sick.	
	26/10/17		Parades:- 9- 9.30 S.O's Inspection 9.30-10.30 Squad Drill 10.45-11.45 Bayonet Drill 11.45- 12.15pm Arms Cleaning. Orders received from Division to the effect that the Coy. would be attached to the 76th Division from 27/10/17. Orders received that one Section would move to MOYENNEVILLE on 27? O.C. Coy left camp to report to 76th Divn H.Q. at 3pm.	
	27/10/17		Parades:- 9am S.O's Inspection 8.45am Capt Sexton paraded full strength with limbers and marched via BOIRY to MOYENNEVILLE. O.C. Coy joined No.1 Section at MOYENNEVILLE.	

Army Form C. 2118.

WAR DIARY
or
INTELLIGENCE SUMMARY.
(Erase heading not required.)

Instructions regarding War Diaries and Intelligence Summaries are contained in F. S. Regs., Part II. and the Staff Manual respectively. Title pages will be prepared in manuscript.

Place	Date	Hour	Summary of Events and Information	Remarks and references to Appendices
FIELD	28/10/17		10.10 am Church Parade. O.C. Coy moving up line with Bn. later.	
			to reconnoitre of day barrage emplacements for 1 Section at ????? in line	
			Strength:- O.9 O.R. 165 Attached O.R. 26 1 O.R. evacuated sick	
	29/10/17		Parades:- 9-9.30 am L.O.s Inspection 9.30-10.30 Squad Drill	
			10.45-11.45 Care & Cleaning 11.45-12.30 Picking Limbers	
	30/10/17		Parades:- 9-9.30 Inspection by I.O's 9.30-10-30 Squad Drill 10.45-11.45 Barrage	
			Drill 11.45-12.30 pm Care & Cleaning	
			Strength:- O.9 O.R. 160 Attached O.R. 26.	
			O.C. Coy. returned to HENDECOURT CAMP.	
	31/10/17		Parades:- Inspection by I.Os 9-9.30, 9.30-10.30 Squad Drill, 10.45-11.45	
			Barrage Drill 11.45-12.30 Care & Cleaning	
			Strength:- O.9 O.R. 161 O.R. attached 26 1 O.R. rejoined from Hospital	

A6945 Wt. W14142/M1160 350,000 12/16 D. D. & L. Forms/C./2118/14.

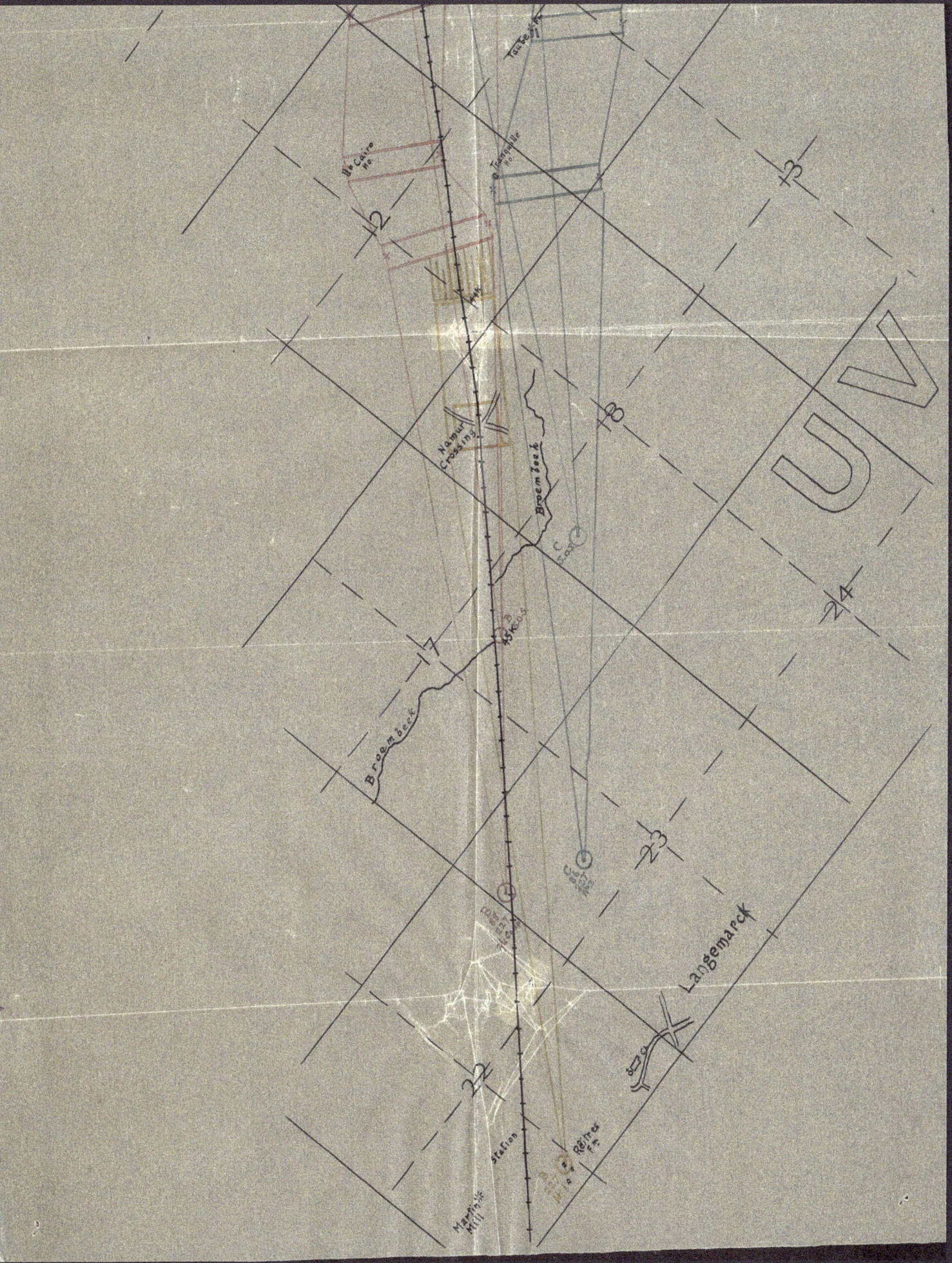

CONFIDENTIAL

War Diary
of
227 Coy. Machine Gun Corps

From 1/11/17
To. 30/11/17

(Volume V.)

D.T./9a
No 15

From:- O.C 227 Coy
            M.G.C
To:-   D.H.Q
            29th Division

Herewith original War Diary
(Volume V) for November 1917.

                                J. Hudson, Captain,
                        Comdg. 227 Machine Gun Coy. M.G.C.

Army Form C. 2.

WAR DIARY
or
INTELLIGENCE SUMMARY.
(Erase heading not required.)

Instructions regarding War Diaries and Intelligence Summaries are contained in F. S. Regs., Part II. and the Staff Manual respectively. Title pages will be prepared in manuscript.

Place	Date	Hour	Summary of Events and Information	Remarks and references to Appendices
Field	1/11/17		Parades 9-9.30 Inspection by S.O's 9.30-10.30 Squad Drill 10.45-11.45 Elementary Gun Drill. 11.45-12.30 Care & Cleaning One Officer & 15 O.R. taken on Strength Strength O.10 O.6. 176 attached O.R. 26	
	2/11/17		Parades 9-9.30 Inspection 9.30-10.30 Company Drill 10.45-11.45 Barrage Drill 11.45-12.30 Care & Cleaning. General H. & S.O's visited No 1 Ration in line to see Barrage positions	
	3/11/17		Parades 9-9.30 Inspection by S.O's 9.30-11.45 Route march 12 months.	
	4/11/17		C of E parade for Divine Service at 11.30 am. Gen Cunliffe passed at 10.30 am	
	5/11/17		Parades 9-9.30 Inspection by S.O.b 9.30-10.30 Company Drill 10.45-11.45 Combined Drill 11.45-12.30 Preparation of Lewis Gunnery fire from gun. No 1 Ration returned from line to HENDECOURT at 9.30 pm	

Army Form C. 2118.

WAR DIARY
or
INTELLIGENCE SUMMARY.
(Erase heading not required.)

Instructions regarding War Diaries and Intelligence Summaries are contained in F. S. Regs., Par. II. and the Staff Manual respectively. Title pages will be prepared in manuscript.

Place	Date	Hour	Summary of Events and Information	Remarks and references to Appendices
FIELD	5/4/17		Parades 9-9.30 Inspection by S.O. 9.30-10.30 Company Drill 10.45-11.45	
			Bayt Guard Drill 11.45-12.30 Care & Cleaning	
			Rgt O.R. O.R.176	Thef
	7/4/17		Parades 9-9.30 Inspection by S.O. 9.30-11.30 Coy Drill 1.45-11.30	
			T.T. 11.30-12.30 Preparation of Army 10.45	
			Rgt O.R. O.R. 100 O.C attached 26	Thef
	8/4/17		2.30am Parade for Baths at Blainville	
			Remainder of morning in support of later Officers	
			Rgt L O.R. O.R. 179 B.G attached 28	Thef
			L.O.R. received and 3rd O.R. awarded Sgt Dumo	Thef
	9/4/17		Parades 9-9.30 S.O. Inspection 9.30-10.30 Squad Drill 10.45	
			10.45 Bombing Drill 11.45-12.30 C.C	Thef
	10/4/17		9-9.30 Inspection 9.30-12.15 Route March	Thef
	11/4/17		Coy Parade for Divine Service 09.10am	Thef

Army Form C. 2118.

WAR DIARY
or
INTELLIGENCE SUMMARY.
(Erase heading not required.)

Instructions regarding War Diaries and Intelligence Summaries are contained in F.S. Regs., Part II. and the Staff Manual respectively. Title pages will be prepared in manuscript.

Place	Date	Hour	Summary of Events and Information	Remarks and references to Appendices
HENDICOURT	12th Nov.		Training. 8.M.	
do.	13th Nov.		Training. 8.M.	
do.	14th Nov.		Fraizingien Battege drill. 8.M. Capt. W.G. Hudson M.C. takes over command of company. M.M.	
do.	15th Nov.	9 am - 1 pm.	Tactical scheme carried out by division in the neighbourhood of RANSART. This scheme was a practice for the offensive near CAMBRAI, and was watched by the Commander-in-Chief. S.M.	
do.	16th Nov.		Secret concentration commenced. Transport moves by night to BAPAUME. S.M.	
do.	17th Nov.		Company entrained with 86th Inf. Bde. at BOISLEUX-au-MONT at 10.30 am.	
HAUT ALLAINES	18th Nov.		C.O. Company detrained at PERONNE at 5 am; and marched to HAUT ALLAINES where the Transport rejoined. S.M. 6 mi Coy. marches to Staging Area (F/NS) and transport to SOREL + LE-GRAND.	

Army Form C. 2118.

WAR DIARY
or
INTELLIGENCE SUMMARY.
(Erase heading not required.)

Place	Date	Hour	Summary of Events and Information	Remarks and references to Appendices
FINS	Nov 15th		Stores area. Cooks and blankets loaded in to stores. Pack-animals loaded and at 2 a.m. company joins in column according to the assembly area, 1 mile west of GOUZEAUCOURT.	
	Nov 20th		Zero at 5.40 a.m. III Corps with IV Corps on left attacked German defensive system between BANTEUX and RIBECOURT. At 11 am Bugle announced that the 12th, 20th, 6th divisions (right to left) had captured the first two objectives. The 29th division which at ZERO advanced from the Assembly Area to our original front line by VILLERS PLUICH, passed through, the 86th Bde (to which No 1 section was attached) attacked and captured MASNIERES, the 87th Bde captured MARCOING, and accomplished the high ground North of ST. QUENTIN CANAL, the 88th Bde captured the dominating ground at NINE WOOD. The canal bridges were intact (except at MASNIERES which was broken by a tank), and the cavalry passed through. N° 2 and 3 section consolidated sunken m. ridge south and parallel to canal. S.M. Casualties Nil.	

Army Form C. 2118.

WAR DIARY
or
INTELLIGENCE SUMMARY.
(Erase heading not required.)

Place	Date	Hour	Summary of Events and Information	Remarks and references to Appendices
MARCOING	Nov. 21st		Consolidation of captured ground carried out. Coy. H.Q. established at MARCOING CHATEAU, also transport. Casualties Nil. 9M.	
do.	Nov. 22nd		Situation normal. Casualties Nil. 9M.	
do.	Nov. 23rd		Situation normal. Barrage lines laid out to cover front. Casualties Nil. 8M.	
do.	Nov. 24th		Situation normal. Wounded 1 O.R. 9M.	
do.	Nov. 25th		Situation normal. Casualties nil. 8M.	
do.	Nov. 26th		do. 8M.	
do.	Nov. 27th		do. 4M.	
do.	Nov. 28th		do. 8M.	

Army Form C. 2118.

WAR DIARY
or
INTELLIGENCE SUMMARY.
(Erase heading not required.)

Instructions regarding War Diaries and Intelligence Summaries are contained in F. S. Regs., Part II. and the Staff Manual respectively. Title pages will be prepared in manuscript.

Place	Date	Hour	Summary of Events and Information	Remarks and references to Appendices
MARCOING	Nov. 29th		German artillery very active, also considerable hostile aerial activity. Transport sent back to SOREL. Casualties Nil.	
			S/M.	
do.	Nov. 30th	4:30 a.m.	Hostile gas shelling of MARCOING and MASNIÈRES.	
		4 - 8.30 a.m.	Heavy bombardment of our positions and villages.	
		7 a.m.	Hostile attack on MASNIÈRES repulsed. 20th division on our right flank fell back, LES RUES VERTES captured by enemy and recaptured by 86th A.B. Enemy advance on MARCOING checked by counter-attack of 88th Inf. Bde. 6 guns of this unit under 2/Lt. W. Richards check enemy advance on WELSH RIDGE and knock out 4 German machine guns coming into VERTES action against 88th Inf. Bde. Positions north of canal attack 4 machine guns in LES RUES Collected during operations Nov. 30th – Dec. 4th Officers: Missing 2, O.R.s 4.5, 8 machine guns.	
			S/M.	

CONFIDENTIAL

WAR DIARY.

OF

227 MACHINE GUN COMPANY.

(Volume VI)

FROM 1/10/17. TO 31/12/17.

From:— O.C. 227 Coy
                    M.G.C.

To:— D.H.Q.
         29th Division

Forward original War Diary for
December 1917.

G. Hudson, Captain,
Comdg. 227 Machine Gun Coy. M.G.C.

Army Form C. 2118.

WAR DIARY
or
INTELLIGENCE SUMMARY.
(Erase heading not required.)

Place	Date	Hour	Summary of Events and Information	Remarks and references to Appendices
MARCOING	1st Dec.		During the night the line was reorganised. The morning was quiet, but at 3 pm the enemy put down a heavy barrage on MASNIÈRES and retook LES RUES VERTES. Orders were issued for the evacuation of MASNIÈRES by the 86th Bde., during the night. This was accomplished, strong patrols on the bridge over the ST. QUENTIN CANAL and machine guns covered this withdrawal. The new line ran about 400× E. of MARCOING COPSE. During the 30th Nov. and Dec. 1st the company lost 8 guns, O.R. missing and killed 45. Officers Wounded and missing; 2nd Lt. J.B. HILL Missing; 2nd Lt. J.H. Kinahan. J.N.	
do.	2nd Dec.		About 8 am a German battalion was seen advancing into MASNIÈRES and was fired at and dispersed. During the night the 87th Inf. Bde. was relieved N.W. of the ST QUENTIN CANAL and marched out on relief by 16th Inf. Bde., the subsection of No 2 section went to RIBÉCOURT. Casualties Nil. J.N.	

Army Form C. 2118.

WAR DIARY
or
INTELLIGENCE SUMMARY.
(Erase heading not required.)

Instructions regarding War Diaries and Intelligence Summaries are contained in F. S. Regs., Part II, and the Staff Manual respectively. Title pages will be prepared in manuscript.

Place	Date	Hour	Summary of Events and Information	Remarks and references to Appendices
MARCOING	3rd Dec		Morning quiet. At 12 noon enemy opened a heavy bombardment on positions of 88th Bde. in support E. of MARCOING COPSE, along the valley to MARCOING, and on both sides of the ST. QUENTIN CANAL. 1 P.M. attack, the enemy gained a foothold in the front line of the 88th Bde. and the attacked and drove the 16th Bde. back to the banks of the canal. A line was consolidated through MARCOING along the edge of the canal to TALMA CHATEAU and up to BROWNLINE. Casualties Nil.	
do	4th Dec		A quiet day. During the night the 29th Div. was relieved by the 36th Div. An order arrived about 6 p.m. to withdraw to the HINDENBURG LINE. Company on relief marches to FINS.	
FINS	5th Dec		Company entrains at 11 a.m. with 81st Bde. at ETRICOURT, detrains at 5 p.m. at MONDICOURT and marches to GRAND ROULLECOURT. Transport marches to BAPAUME.	

WAR DIARY
or
INTELLIGENCE SUMMARY.
(Erase heading not required.)

Army Form C. 2118.

Place	Date	Hour	Summary of Events and Information	Remarks and references to Appendices
GRAND ROULLECOURT	6th Dec.		Cleaning Up. Transport moves to COUTURELLE. S.M.	
do.	7th Dec.		Company marches to DENIER. Transport rejoins unit. S.M.	
DENIER	8th Dec.		Cleaning guns, ammunition, etc. S.M.	
do.	9th Dec.		Training. Church parade. S.M.	
do.	10th Dec.		Training. Gun drills, gas drills, lectures, stoppages, squadrills, etc. S.M.	
do.	11th Dec.		Inspection of Coy. by O.C. S.M.	
do.	12th Dec.		Training. S.M.	
do.	13th Dec.		Training. S.M.	
do.	14th Dec.		Training. Battn. S.M.	
do.	15th Dec.		Training. S.M.	
do.	16th Dec.		Divine Service. S.M.	
do.	17th Dec.		Coy. marches to BAVINCOURT. Heavy snowfall impedes march. S.M.	

WAR DIARY
or
INTELLIGENCE SUMMARY.
(Erase heading not required.)

Army Form C. 2118.

Place	Date	Hour	Summary of Events and Information	Remarks and references to Appendices
BLANGERM	18th Dec		Coy. marches to VIEIL HESDIN, transport accompanies unit. Roads frozen and covered up. S.M.	
VIEIL HESDIN	19th Dec		Coy. marches to FRUGES, transport to BIMNT. S.M.	
FRUGES	20th Dec		Coy. marches to CLENLEU, rejoined by transport. S.M.	
CLENLEU	21st Dec		Cleaning up guns, equipments etc. S.M.	
do	22nd Dec		Training S.M.	
do	23rd Dec		Route March S.M.	
do	24th Dec		Training S.M.	
do	25th Dec		Church parade S.M.	
do	26th Dec		Clearing road to HUCQUELIERS of snow. S.M.	
do	27th Dec		Route March S.M.	
do	28th Dec		Training S.M. Inspection by O.C.	
do	29th Dec		Training S.M.	
do	30th Dec		Church parade S.M.	
do	31st Dec		Training, Loading pack animals etc. S.M.	

Army Form C. 2118.

WAR DIARY
or
INTELLIGENCE SUMMARY.
(Erase heading not required.)

Instructions regarding War Diaries and Intelligence Summaries are contained in F. S. Regs., Part II. and the Staff Manual respectively. Title pages will be prepared in manuscript.

Place	Date	Hour	Summary of Events and Information	Remarks and references to Appendices
Aubin	Jan 1st 1916	9.30 – 12.30 pm	Route March PM:G	
	Jan 2nd		Church.	
		9.30 – 11 am	When Coming & Packing limbers ready for track.	
		12.30 pm	T.O.R examined 9	
			through Officer. T.O.R. 170 PM:G	
	Jan 3rd		Training PM:G	
	Jan 4th		Coy turned out 6 am & marched org. Wagon to Werthiecourt. Billets taken over in clean condition. PM:G	
Withiecourt	Jan 5th		Training	

Army Form C. 2118.

WAR DIARY
or
INTELLIGENCE SUMMARY.
(Erase heading not required.)

Instructions regarding War Diaries and Intelligence
Summaries are contained in F. S. Regs., Part II.
and the Staff Manual respectively. Title pages
will be prepared in manuscript.

Place	Date	Hour	Summary of Events and Information	Remarks and references to Appendices
Whitwick Post Off.	Jan 6th		Parade for Pay 11.0 a.m. Strength Officers 10 O.R. 170 NCO's	
	Jan 7th	9.0 – 12.15 pm 2.0 – 4.0 pm	Training Drills NCO's	
	Jan 8th	9 – 12.30	Training 1 O.R. Corporals Cub Strength Officers 10 O.R. 169 NCO's	
	Jan 9th	9.0 – 12.30	Training 2 O.R. evacuated sick Strength Officers 10 O.R. 167 NCO's	

Army Form C. 2118.

WAR DIARY
or
INTELLIGENCE SUMMARY.
(Erase heading not required.)

Instructions regarding War Diaries and Intelligence Summaries are contained in F. S. Regs., Part II. and the Staff Manual respectively. Title pages will be prepared in manuscript.

Place	Date	Hour	Summary of Events and Information	Remarks and references to Appendices
Whitechurch Park	Jan 10th		9.0 – 12.30 Training A.M.G	
	Jan 11th		9.0 – 12.30pm Training Awards.	
			T/Lt W Richards awarded Military Cross	
			152204 C.S.M. Ellison Distinguished Conduct Medal	
			44558 Cpl W.J. Dudley M.M. A.M.G	
	Jan 12th		9.0 – 12.30 Rangework	
			L.O.R. posted from same	
			Strength O.R. 10	
			O.R. 186 A.M.G	
	Jan 13th		Church Parade A.M.G	

WAR DIARY
or
INTELLIGENCE SUMMARY.
(Erase heading not required.)

Army Form C. 2118.

Place	Date	Hour	Summary of Events and Information	Remarks and references to Appendices
Blackhurst	Jan 14th	9.0 a.m. - 12.30 p.m.	Training. A.H.E.G	
	Jan 15th		Preparing to move in accordance with enclosed order. A.H.E.G	
	Jan 16th		Coy paraded at 6.45 a.m. & marched via Dunkirk to Wizerne where it entrained for Brandhoek arriving about 3.6 pm. 2 O.R. taken on Strength from Base. Strength O 10 O.R. 170 A.H.E.G	
Brandhoek Siding			Coy paraded 3 pm and moved to Ypres. A.H.E.G	

WAR DIARY
or
INTELLIGENCE SUMMARY.

Army Form C. 2118.

(Erase heading not required.)

Place	Date	Hour	Summary of Events and Information	Remarks and references to Appendices
Hens	18/5	9.P.30	Cleaning Gun Kit. S.M.G	
	19/5	9.12.30	Cy prepared Gun Kit for line S.M.G	
	20/5	3.15 am	3 sections relieved sections of 28th M.G. Cy in barrage positions in Brocklindale sector. 1 section relieved section of 28th M.G. Cy in defense position. S.M.G	
	21/5		Situation normal. Casualties - nil. S.M.G	
	22/5		Heavily shelled with gas at Hem. Casualties - nil S.M.G	
	23/5		Situation normal - Casualties - nil S.M.G	
	24/5		8 guns moved to London Ridge. Cy headquarters H.Q at Hem. Rear H.Q. and 8 reserve guns moved to Millif. Casualties - nil S.M.G	

Army Form C. 2118.

WAR DIARY
or
INTELLIGENCE SUMMARY.
(Erase heading not required.)

Place	Date	Hour	Summary of Events and Information	Remarks and references to Appendices
Hulluch	25th Jan.		Positions on London Ridge shelled with H.E. Shrapnel. Casualties - nil.	J.H.Y.
	26.		Situation - normal. Casualties - nil.	J.H.Y.
	27		2 E.A. engaged with M.G. fire from position near fork. Casualties - nil.	J.H.Y.
	28		Gun Positions shelled with light gas shells for 10 mins at 5 a.m. Casualties - nil.	J.H.Y.
	29		Situation normal. Casualties - nil.	J.H.Y.
	30		Situation normal. Casualties - nil.	J.H.Y.

WAR DIARY
or
INTELLIGENCE SUMMARY.

227 M.G. Coy. Army Form C. 2118.

9 of 7

Place	Date	Hour	Summary of Events and Information	Remarks and references to Appendices
Vielle	June 3		Situation normal. Casualties – nil	
			Strife	

F. Hudson, Captain,
Comdg. 227 Machine Gun Coy. M.G.C.